PORTAL TO FLORIDA'S PAST

AN ARCHAEOLOGY ADVENTURE

TOUR STARTS HERE

BY AMY A. ELDER   ILLUSTRATED BY GARRY WALTER

the Peppertree Press
Sarasota, Florida

This book is dedicated to
Amy Walter
(Cindy and Garry's daughter)
and
Connor Elder Keane
(Amy's son)

Acknowledgment

We would like to acknowledge Historic Spanish Point; including Linda Mansperger, Kara Pallin, Ryan Murphy and numerous volunteers who work to preserve and protect this beautiful museum. We appreciate Cindy Walter for being our technical advisor. We would also like to thank our families and friends who helped us along the way, including the National League of American Pen Women writers group who helped critique the story, Betsy and Doug Elder and Mary and Rick Thayer for being my cheerleaders, and to Linda Campbell, Caroline Reed, and my kind husband David Keane for their support. Thanks to our friends from Scrambles Café and Café Bentley's for providing our gathering places in Osprey, Florida, and to the native animals and people from Florida's past and the people who help pass on their story. A special thank-you goes to Pine View School, vice principal Lisa Wheatley, and especially Mrs. Congero's fourth-grade classes and Mrs. Shea's third-grade class, and the Out-of-Door Academy fifth-grade students. Their questions, input and evaluations were a valuable resource for reviewing this book.

For information regarding permission, call 941-922-2662 or contact us at our website:
www.peppertreepublishing.com or write to: the Peppertree Press, LLC. Attention: Publisher
1269 First Street, Suite 7, Sarasota, Florida 34236

ISBN: 978-1-61493-134-8
Library of Congress Number: 2012920611
Printed in the U.S.A.
First printing January 2013
Second printing August 2013

THIS BOOK BELONGS TO

Table of Contents

FLORIDA'S ANCIENT PEOPLE

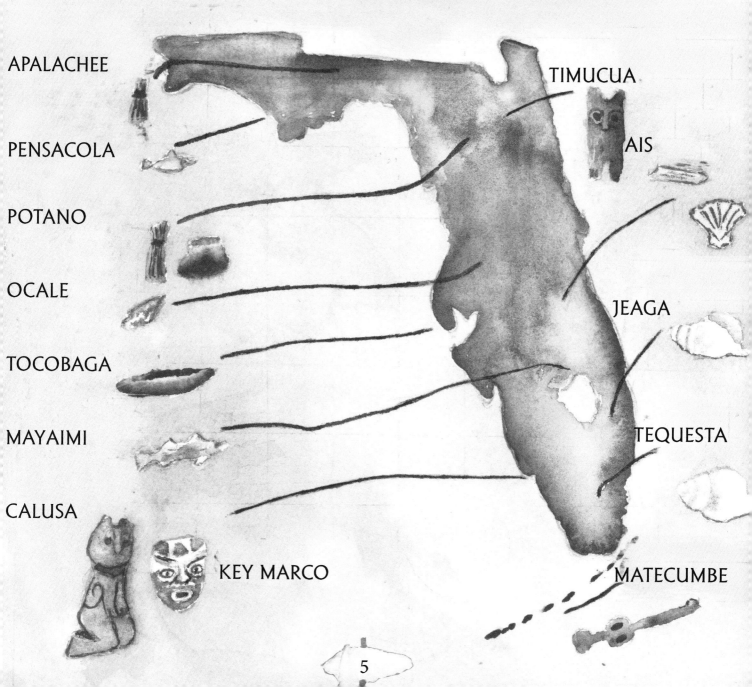

APALACHEE

PENSACOLA

POTANO

OCALE

TOCOBAGA

MAYAIMI

CALUSA

TIMUCUA

AIS

JEAGA

TEQUESTA

KEY MARCO

MATECUMBE

TIMELINE
(In Years Ago)

14,000 - 8,000	8,000 - 7,000	7,000 - 4,000	4,000 -3,200	3,200 - 1,000	1,000 - 500	500
Paleo-Indian	Early Archaic	Middle Archaic	Late Archaic	Woodland	Mississippian	Contact
Florida is cold and twice the size. Sea level 180 to 300 feet lower. Traveled in small bands. Dryer climate. Hunted mammoths, bison and camel.	Shell, bone and stone tools in use. Hardwood forests cover state.	Population stationary and making better tools. Sea level at present day level. Middens begin.	Beginning of making fire-tempered pottery. Pine forests begin growing due to a moist climate.	Improved pottery technology, creates stronger pottery. Communities develop with a system of politics and religion.	Communication between cultures increasing, with the sharing of ideas. Chiefdoms. Bow and arrow in use.	Spanish arrive bringing disease and culture changes, (such as religion).

Definitions: Archaic - Very old, as it relates to a primitive time period.
Chiefdom - A complex society led by an individual.

Sources: Florida Department of State, Division of Historical Resources.National Park Service.
Florida's First People by Robin Brown.
Timeline by Garry Walter/cpw

Chapter 1
PORTAL

"Welcome to our Florida museum. My spirit name is *Alligator with Large Pointy Teeth* but you can call me Al. I'll be your tour guide. We will be going through a portal to the past and exploring Florida's rich history. You will learn to live at peace with nature and others."

"**Archaeologists** discovered that **prehistoric** people first lived in Florida 12,500 years ago. We will see the traces they left and the plants they used. Native plants are good for the environment. They are drought and heat resistant and provide shelter, oxygen, and food. They flourish here, and we will see them as we walk," Al hands everyone a portal ticket for admission to an **archaeology** adventure. Through a mysterious **mangrove** mist, they go over a walkway and enter a portal to the past, and a magical thing happens! As he speaks, Al turns into an American alligator with large pointy teeth. In this mysterious, magical museum, the animals, reptiles, and birds can talk!

A lively boy with red hair and freckles asks, "Do we get to turn into an animal too?"

"That's a good question. Your question will be answered at the end of the tour. Since you are curious, I will give you the spirit name, *Curious Armadillo*. As we go on this journey together I will assign spirit names that suit each of you," Al promises the group.

"My family has been around for a long time. They came to North America with the **Paleoindians**. During the Ice Age, dating back 14,000 years, people came to the Americas from Siberia. They followed many animals, which are extinct today, including mammoths, mastodons, saber-tooth tigers and large sloths. Now stay on the path so my friends don't mistake you for lunch!" Al smiled, showing off his large pointy teeth.

A petite girl with glasses and almond-green eyes said, "This is confusing. Why did we go back in time?"

"Another good question. Your spirit name will be *Clever Cat*. Now to answer your question. The best way to show you history is to live it. The portal brought us back in time. No worries. As long as you stay on the path and follow my directions, I will return you to the present, and you can get on the bus at the end of the day," Al said.

When they finished walking, they ended up at a beautiful pond.

"Over to the left you will see a fresh water pond, a **natural resource**. That's the reason my family moved here and why the **prehistoric** people could live here," Al said.

"Wait a minute. My ancestors lived here when the **prehistoric** people first came here 12,500 years ago. I should tell the story," Turtle protested.

"If you insist. This is Turtle and she will be your tour guide," Al said.

Turtle stretched her neck as far as she could and said, "I'm a Gopher tortoise."

"**Archaeologists** have determined there were **prehistoric** people living here from the mounds they left behind. Other people have lived here as well. **Calusa** and Tocobaga Indians, Spaniards, Cuban fishermen and pioneers all lived here, partly because they had fresh water to drink. This pond is now home to many animals, reptiles and birds."

"Al, where are you going next?" Turtle asked before retreating into her shell.

"We are continuing the tour. Next we are going to the **Burial Mound**," Al cleared his throat.

"Can I come?" Turtle asked.

"You're too slow!" Al grunted.

"Can I jump on your back?" Turtle pleaded.

"OK, hurry up," Al closed his eyes and enjoyed the tropical sun.

Turtle jumped on Al's back, and they swaggered off to the **Burial Mound**.

ACTIVITY: WORD SEARCH
Find the Glossary Words

```
K D A S J F J L H M W G T E E T C I M C M O S M
P A L E O I N D I A N S T D C N Z O T A A S T O
M A Z R D K E C L C I A U X R E I U V Q N P C T
A L L Z E X C I L G M G Q B U I W U V D G Z A S
Q S J E T A S U O I O O P B O C F D Y G R X F U
A H C I O S I L L U B A G U S N D W B V O A I C
W S N I O N O C T T L B R R E A V G Q O V C T I
T C U F R E T C A M U C I I R Y Y B L P E W R Y
T O E L A O A O E K R R D A L C A Y D T S A R
N B O H A N T T L I N M E L A D E C O R D A G E
R C C L O C T S E O E U N M R I Q R H R Y S C E
T R J E S O J A I N G M L O U G L U E U G G Y W
A M I D D E N P T H I Y D U T S T H K M Y E T G
T N E M N O R I V N E L M N A I S O W K O A X W
P R E S E R V E D N N R E D N T F C T G Y N I W
L E V E L A E S V X S L P M O E L T A L T A Y E
X W Q S F J W X Y H A D S P I D P N N Y L I F T
O L R F C E O L U E M E M V X T F W P U X T B H
```

ANCIENT   ARCHAEOLOGIST   ARTIFACTS   ATLATL
BURIAL MOUND   CALUSA   CEREMONY   CLIMATE
CORDAGE   CULTURE   CUSTOM   DIGSITE
DUGOUT CANOE   ENVIRONMENT   EXTINCT   FOSSIL
GRID   HUT   MANGROVE   MIDDEN
NATURAL RESOURCE   PALEOINDIANS   PALEONTOLOGY   PALMETTO
POTSHERDS   PREHISTORIC   PRESERVED   SEA LEVEL
TIMELINE   TOOLS

BURIAL
MOUND

12

Chapter 2
BURIAL MOUND

"Here is the **Burial Mound**," Al gestured.

"Hold on. My ancestors lived here when the native people first came. I should tell the story," Owl interrupted, blinking her round eyes.

"If you insist. This is Owl, and she will be your tour guide if she can stay awake. Aren't you nocturnal? I thought you were supposed to sleep during the day and hunt at night?" Al yawned.

Owl fluttered her wings in excitement and replied, "I'm an Eastern Screech owl. Yes, I took a nap so I could be here for the tour. This is a sand **burial mound** dating back from 1700 to 1100 years ago. In the early 1960s, **archaeologists** found skeletons of humans and dogs, potsherds and shell tools here. The **prehistoric** people were buried with their possessions as an offering to their ancestors. Just seven inches from the surface, they found sawfish vertebrae beads, pots and even an alligator. Sorry, Al."

"That's creepy," shuttered a tall boy who was always in the front of the group.

"I'll say. Who would want an alligator for a pet?" Al said and smiled at the tall dark-haired boy as the sun gleams off his big teeth.

"Your spirit name will be *Brave Florida Panther*. The **prehistoric** people thought alligators would protect them from danger in the afterlife."

"The **archaeologists** estimate there are still bodies buried in the mound," Owl said. "Where are you going now?"

"To the Student **Dig Site**," Al said.

"Can I come?" Owl asked.

"OK, we will meet you there," Al replied.

Owl flew off to the Student **Dig Site**, while Al and Turtle swaggered off to meet her.

ACTIVITY: CROSSWORD PUZZLE

Across

2. Rope, cord or twine made from natural fibers
3. Something people use, like water
9. Scientist who studies artifacts
12. An area separated by lines to form squares
13. A way of life
17. Pieces of broken pottery
18. Preserved ancient animal remains
20. Special event or custom to celebrate together
21. Area used by archaeologists to learn about the past

Down

1. Resource, something in nature people can use
4. No longer living
5. Circular homes built by prehistoric people
6. Tropical trees that live on coastal shores
7. Holds a spear, used for hunting
8. Used by archaeologists to dig and measure
10. Weather pattern of an area
11. The way people do things in a group
13. Lived in Florida 1600-400 years ago
14. A trash heap
15. A time before history was recorded
16. The height of the ocean's surface
19. Place where a collection of objects is preserved

Chapter 3
STUDENT DIG SITE

"Here's a **dig site** that was built for students to explore and dig for **artifacts**. Before we get started, I have to remind you that all **artifacts** and materials found here are part of our **museum** collection. I'm sorry, but you can't take anything with you. We need to help **preserve** this special place I call home," Al said.

"Al, I know the story. My family has lived here since the Europeans came in the 1500s. I should be able to tell the story," Lizard begged.

"If you insist. Everyone, this is Lizard and he will be your tour guide," Al said.

Lizard puffed out his neck in excitement, did a few push-ups, and began. "I am a Green Anole lizard. This is the Student **Dig Site**. This is my favorite thing to do, and I hope at the end of the day it will be one of yours as well. Today we will all become **archaeologists** and dig for **artifacts**. Who likes to dig in the dirt?" Lizard asked.

Everyone's hand went up.

"Good. First I'll explain the different categories of **artifacts,** and then you will be able to dig for them," Lizard said. "I have three rows of **artifacts**, which consist of shell **tools**, **potsherds** and animal remains. Each row represents a category that we will be looking for when we dig today," Lizard explained.

"The first row is made of **shell tools**. These whelk and clam shells were used for **tools**. Since we didn't have **tool** stores, the native people used their **natural resources**.

See how they drilled a hole and inserted a stick to make a hammer in this whelk shell and the clam shell can be used as a scraper," Lizard indicated.

"The second row is **potsherds**, which are broken pieces of pottery. The **ancient** people first made pottery by forming clay in circular layers. When they added fiber to the pottery, they learned they needed to make it thicker because the fiber would burn off. They eventually found that adding sand to the mixture made the pottery stronger."

"The last row contains animal remains. To survive, the people who lived here had to use animals for food, clothing, and **tools**. Since they hunted mostly with a spear and an **atlatl**, they tried to use as much as possible from the animal. For example, if they caught a deer they ate the meat, used the skins for clothes and warmth and used the jaw for a knife. Other animal remains in the site are sharks teeth, vertebrate, fossilized bones, antlers, and turtle shells. We can tell how old the **artifacts** are by using a process called carbon-14 dating. They use it to determine the ages of objects like wood, cloth, bone and plant fiber as far back as 50,000 years ago." Lizard moved aside to let the students have a closer look.

Lizard inflated his throat. "You remember the three categories I showed you. There is another category: unknown. It's where more investigating is done once you've left the **dig site**."

Lizard weaves around the **dig site** and lands on a whelk shell. "See the hole in this? This was used as a shell tool." He moves around to a fossilized bone. "This is a fossilized rib of a manatee." Finally he lands on the third roped area of the site. "This is an animal remain. Once we find the **artifacts**, we use a sifting screen to get the excess dirt out, leaving the small **artifacts** exposed for examination. Then we clean and record what we find."

"Al, where are you going now?" Lizard asked.

"Now that the students have accomplished their training, we will go to an Active **Dig Site**," Al said.

"Can I come?" Lizard asked.

"OK, jump on my back," Al smiled, and they all went on their way.

ACTIVE
DIGSITE

18

ACTIVITY: ARTIFACT SCAVENGER HUNT

Can you find these items in the Student Dig Site?

1. Shell hammer
2. Shell scraper
3. Potsherd
4. Jaw bone
5. Turtle shell
6. Antler
7. Shark tooth
8. Fish vertebrae

ACTIVE DIGSITE

NOTES

20

Chapter 4
ACTIVE DIG SITE

"Here we can see **artifacts** from an Active **Dig Site** that are currently being investigated," Al said.

A small voice interrupted, "Excuse me, I'm down here. My family lived here about 2,000 years ago. I should tell the story." Off to one side sat a spider, not too pleased to have so many intruders.

Spider carefully placed her eight legs over a string of vertebrates and said, "I'm a Black Widow spider. You can identify me by the hourglass on my belly. Don't get too near, my bite can make you sick. **Archaeologists** have discovered clues to an **ancient** community that once lived in Florida and the **natural resources** used to help them survive. Through layers of shell, ash, soil and post molds, they can determine what they ate, how they cooked their food, made pottery and tools, and what their homes looked like."

Two boys stood off to the side chasing each other. They were wearing Florida football-team hats. One boy who successfully stole his friend's Buccaneer hat asked, "What's a post mold?"

"Good question. Your spirit name will be *Chasing Osprey*. A post mold is a place in the ground where a dark

circle appears. It usually has a diameter of one to eight inches. This is evidence showing where a post supporting a palmetto hut was pushed down into the ground." Al peered at the boys with interest.

Another boy wearing a Seminole sports hat asked, "What did the homes look like?"

"Your name will be *Running Horse*," Al said. "Spider, please continue."

As Spider scurries around the site, she feels the ground shaking. She lands on a sharks tooth and in a quivering voice says, "They were round and usually made of palm fronds and natural items found on the land."

Just then, a mist rose from the ground and a palmetto hut appeared in the **dig site**.

A tall boy wearing braces whistled through his teeth as he spoke, "Wow! Is that a palmetto hut from the past?"

"Yes." Al bellowed. "Your spirit name will be *Hissing Snake*. Look class here's an **atlatl**."

"What a magical place! And what's an **atlatl**?" A slight boy ducking in and out of the group asked.

"Your spirit name will be *Vanishing Bobcat*," Al said. "An **atlatl** is a spear launcher used to throw spears that the native people used to hunt food. Look and see the vision of a village. You can see the chief throwing a spear with an **atlatl**, a woman burning the wood fibers of a log, then scraping the ashes with a clam shell scraper to make a **dugout** canoe and a young boy starting a fire with a bow drill."

"Al, where are you going next?" Spider asked.

"To the Late Archaic **Midden**," Al said.

"Can I come?" Spider asked.

"You're too slow!" Al grunted.

"Then I will bring her," Owl said.

They all started off to the Late Archaic **Midden**. Al, Turtle and Lizard marched by land and Owl and Spider flew high into the clouds. From her perspective in the sky, Spider thought the large live oaks draped in Spanish moss looked like old men's beards blowing in the tropical breeze.

ACTIVITY: TOOL SCAVENGER HUNT

Can you find these items in the Active Dig Site?

1. What device on a tripod would be used to map a dig site?

2. This is used to sift for small artifacts.

3. Used to remove soil from an artifact.

4. Used for finer cleaning of an artifact.

5. Used for measuring the size of an artifact.

6. This is what you write on.

7. This is what you write with.

8. Used when you are thirsty.

9. Show you studied archaeology.

AERIAL VIEW

SH
R

Chapter 5
SHELL RING

"This is a Late Archaic **Midden** in the shape of a circle or ring. Late Archaic **Midden** means really old," Al said.

"Now, as you know, my family's lived here since the **Calusa** people at least 1500 years ago. I should tell the story," Butterfly interjected.

"If you insist. This is Butterfly, and he will be your tour guide," Al said.

"I'm a Zebra Longwing butterfly, the Florida state butterfly. Does anyone know what a **midden** is?" Butterfly flipped his striped wings and began.

A girl wearing a purple headband in the back row swiftly put up her hand and answered. "It's a trash heap."

"Very good. A **midden** is a trash heap, which consists of layers of discarded shells, dirt, ash, and animal bones. **Archaeologists** have determined people first lived here about 4,000 years ago. They use **artifacts** to help us understand the **culture** of the people who lived here. With this information, scientists have discovered that people hunted animals, fished, gathered shellfish and berries, and used shells and animal remains for jewelry, tools and musical instruments. From the ash and charcoal, researchers can tell that the people cooked by smoking their fish and meat," Butterfly said. "Al, shall we call her *Swift Bunny?*"

"That would be a fine spirit name for her," Al gave a toothy grin.

"We can tell from the horseshoe shape where the ancient people had their **ceremonial** feasting." Butterfly flapped his wings.

A boy with auburn hair and tan skin talking loudly asked, "If it's shaped like a horseshoe, then why is it called a ring?"

"Your spirit name will be *Powerful Eagle*. Butterfly, will you answer this observant young man's question?" Al asked.

"Originally it was a ring until development destroyed one end and made it a horseshoe. The National Park Service has declared it a Shell Ring," Butterfly said.

Butterfly continued. "There was an abundance of activity until 3200 years ago when **sea levels** dropped. When the **sea level** rose 2500 years ago, people returned. We can tell from the shell ring that they feasted on shellfish such as oysters and scallops for 1200 years. The center was filled with fresh spring water, which brought the people here for **ceremonies**. **Archaeologists** have determined the ring was devoid of **artifacts**," Butterfly said.

A small girl wearing a yellow hat softly asked, "What does devoid of **artifacts** mean?"

"Good question. Listen, *Quiet Deer*, and Butterfly will answer your smart question," Al said.

"It means there are no **artifacts**. In this **midden**, there is no evidence of any tools, because of no outside communications with other people. **Archaeologists** can tell by what is found in a midden when these **ancient** people learned new **customs** from neighboring groups. Al, where are you going next?" Butterfly asked.

"To the Summit **Midden**," Al started slowly walking.

"Can I come?" Butterfly pleaded.

"OK, we'll meet you there," Al said.

ACTIVITY: WORD JUMBLE

Directions: Rearrange the letters of the word to match the definition.

1. The first prehistoric people to live in North and South America, named by archaeologists.

   _ _ _ _ _ _ _ _ _ _ _ _ _   **epadinonlasi**

2. The study of prehistoric life using fossils.

   _ _ _ _ _ _ _ _ _ _ _   **nopatloeogly**

3. Circular homes built by the prehistoric people.

   _ _ _ _ _ _ _ _   _ _ _ _   **meltptao sthu**

4. Pieces of broken pottery found on an archaeological site.

   _ _ _ _ _ _ _ _ _   **stheopsrd**.

5. A time before history was recorded by writing.

   _ _ _ _ _ _ _ _ _ _ _   **tihreprsoic**

6. Kept or Saved. _ _ _ _ _ _ _ _ _   **drepersev**

7. The height of the ocean's surface. _ _ _   _ _ _ _ _   **ase vlele**

8. A diagram that shows events and when they took place.

   _ _ _ _ _ _ _ _   **mitenile**

9. Archaeologists use these to dig and measure. _ _ _ _ _   **sloto**

Answers: Can be found in the glossary.

Chapter 6
SUMMIT MIDDEN

"Here we are at the Summit **Midden**," Al said.

"So, Al, my ancestors have been here since snakes slithered smoothly through the sand," Snake spoke. "I should tell the story."

"If you insist. This is Snake and he will be your tour guide," Al replied.

"I'm a Coral snake, not to be confused with the less powerful King snake. You can identify me by this rhyme, 'Red touching yellow can kill a fellow, red touching black you're okay Jack.'"

"Because I'm poisonous, people like to know how to identify me. Now let's go on with the lesson. This **midden** was built between 2300 years ago and 1700 years ago. There was a change of **cultural** diffusion during this time frame," Snake said.

"What does **cultural** diffusion mean?" a girl in a red-striped shirt who enjoys singing along the tour asked.

"The **ancient** people started changing their customs because of the exchange of ideas with other people," Snake explained.

"Your spirit name is *Singing Cardinal*," Al said. "Snake, please continue."

"**Archaeologists** use the terms summit, shoulder, slope and toe for locating sections of the **midden**. The top of the **midden** is the summit with the most recent trash, the middle is the shoulder and slope, and the bottom is the toe and has the oldest trash," Snake said.

"Al, where are you going now?" Snake asked.

"Well, I'm getting hungry!" Al said, "I'm going to the picnic area for lunch and a story."

"Can I come?" Snake asked.

"You're too slow," Al grunted.

"Then I will bring him with Spider," Owl said.

"Let's go," Turtle said, "We don't want to become lunch!"

They all started off to the picnic area. Al, Turtle, and Lizard sauntered off by land and Owl, Spider, Snake and Butterfly flew high above the ground.

ACTIVITY: NATIVE PLANT SEARCH

Can you find these native plants throughout the book?

1. Catbrier: The native people used the Catbrier plant for food. They used the roots to make a red starch for gravy, bread and pudding.

2. Century plant: The native people used the Century plant for a few different purposes. They would weave the strong fibers and make fishing nets, the sap could be fermented for beverages, and could be used for soap and insecticide.

3. Coontie: The Seminoles called plants that provided starch from wild roots and tubers Coontie, which meant flour-root. The plant had poisonous roots that had to be detoxified to make it safe to cook with.

4. Firebush: The Firebush plant provides food for the Zebra Longwing butterfly. In 1996, Governor Lawton Chiles designated the Zebra Longwing as the Florida state butterfly. The orange-red tubular flowers also supply food for hummingbirds, bees and other insects.

5. Gumbo Limbo tree: The Gumbo Limbo tree is nick-named the tourist tree due to the fact the bark gets red and peels like a tourist without sunscreen. The resin from the tree was used for glue and varnish. The leaves, bark and roots were made into tea and were used to help with illness such as fever.

6. Prickly Pear: The Prickly Pear cactus produces red fruit that was used for food by the native people of Florida. The cactus was used for tea for healing inflammation.

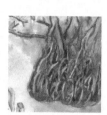

7. Red mangrove: Is one of three mangroves that grow along Florida's coastline. Red, Black and White mangroves are important for the ecosystem providing food and shelter to many aquatic species. It reproduces by sending out long roots which hold them up during storms. The native people would hide their boats in the mangroves for protection during hurricanes.

8. Sabal palm: Also called Cabbage palmetto, is the Florida state tree. The native people made soap, and used fibers to make cordage for nets. They used the fronds for palm-thatched roofs.

9. Spanish Bayonet: The Spanish Bayonet is a shrub found in Florida along shell mounds. The roots were used to make soap, the strong fibers were used to make nets, baskets and shoes and the flower was used in salads.

10. Spanish moss: Spanish moss is part of the Bromeliad family. The flowering plant (not actually a moss) is an epiphyte which means an air plant that gets all the nutrition it needs from the atmosphere and environment. The native people used the fiber to make skirts and added it to pottery for thickening.

CHAPTER 7:
STORYTIME

"Students, please sit crisscross applesauce under the large Ear tree, which is named for its ear-shaped seed pods, while I tell you a story," Al said.

"A long time ago," Al began.

"Pardon me. Since my family's been here since the **ancient** people about 2,000 years ago, I should tell the story," Raccoon complained from up in the tree.

"If you insist. This is Raccoon, and he will tell the story," Al said.

"Now give me your ear, and I will tell you a story from long ago," Raccoon said. "First let me finish the snack I snitched from your lunches! Chocolate chip cookies are my favorite!"

The Midden Builder
by Cindy Walter

There is a famous legend we tell about the most dedicated midden builder of prehistoric Florida. I do not know the name of this most exquisite builder; he lived in a time when there was no written language.

It is said that he was introduced to midden building at a young age, as all small children were. And when he was able to walk, he followed his father with their basket of empty shells and trash to throw into a heap along with others from their village. He enjoyed this chore. To him it had purpose and meaning. It was what their people were known for and was a part of their heritage as fishermen. Besides, he liked seeing the midden get longer and higher day after day.

The little midden builder found that his brothers did not enjoy this chore, so he gladly volunteered to make the extra trips for them. Even when friends wanted to play or practice throwing short spears and pretend to hunt with atlatls, he was happier working on building the midden.

As time went on and the boys were older, they had more grown-up chores, like hunting and fishing. They no longer had time to take trash to the midden. But our builder did not want to stop. He felt much satisfaction from his work and wanted to continue.

The midden builder found that adding dirt between the layers of shells made the midden more stable to walk on. He volunteered to make that step his job, which he happily spent working at day after day. He even asked his mother and sister to make a special pine needle basket woven more tightly to carry the soil.

When the other young men were old enough to have families, they taught their children the skills they learned. Our midden builder was older, too, but he decided he would make constructing the longest, tallest and most solid midden his lifelong work, which he did for many, many years.

As he grew too old to work on the midden, it was decided by all to shut it down. It had gotten quite large and the trip to the top was a very long walk. By now the midden had become really famous. People from all around wanted to come and see this most magnificent creation. No one believed something this special could be made by hand.

While visitors made the journey to the top, our builder watched from below. To see their amazement filled him with pride. No amount of money could compare to his feeling of accomplishment. Before they left, they thanked him for his lifelong dedication. Otherwise, without his hard work, they would never have known such a structure was possible. It brought them much joy and happiness to see.

The visitors learned a valuable lesson that day: if you find something that you are good at and that makes you happy, stick with it. Success in life is measured by doing something meaningful, which also brings you joy. Success is not measured by how much money or how many possessions you have.

The end.

A girl jumping up and down in place asked Al, "Everyone has a spirit name but me. Who will I be?"

"There are lots of native animals to choose from. I think your spirit name should be *Dancing Fox*," Al said.

Curious Armadillo raised his hand and said, "Al, you promised in the beginning of the tour that we would become animals too."

Al replies, "You already have, in spirit."

"You learned what people living here before you were like and how they lived. You also learned what it means to become something greater than yourself and more importantly, how to live in peace with others. I will give you a **Junior Archaeology Certificate** to prove you have completed this class and now are able to appreciate nature." As Al walked across the bridge through the mangroves, he becomes a person again, and they all returned to the present.

The students gathered around Al and thanked him for the tour before boarding the bus.

They all had such a wonderful time; they hoped they would see him again.

As the bus drove off Al saw their new animal spirits leave with them. He was grateful that with the help of the native animal guides, they earned their **Junior Archaeology Certificate**. They could now return to school and teach others what they learned and how to live in peace with nature.

OL BUS

87

YOUR
SPIRIT
LIVES

AL'S RECOMMENDATIONS FOR ANIMAL SPIRIT NAMES

Directions: Choose a first and last name from each category.

NAMES FOR GIRLS

First Name:		Last Name:	
A.	Talking	A.	Jaguar
B.	Wise	B.	Lizard
C.	Serious	C.	Owl
D.	Clever	D.	Wildcat
E.	Patient	E.	Porcupine
F.	Teaching	F.	Raccoon
G.	Clapping	G.	Otter
H.	Skipping	H.	Osprey
I.	Dancing	I.	Crow
J.	Gentle	J.	Pony
K.	Racing	K.	Crane
L.	Swift	L.	Fawn
M.	Quiet	M.	Chameleon
N.	Friendly	N.	Chipmunk
O.	Joyful	O.	Deer
P.	Eager	P.	Gopher
Q.	Beautiful	Q.	Dolphin
R.	Cheerful	R.	Cat
S.	Lively	S.	Fox
T.	Dainty	T.	Cardinal
U.	Mysterious	U.	Mockingbird
V.	Zigzagging	V.	Osprey
W.	Delightful	W.	Blue Jay
X.	Singing	X.	Lamb
Y.	Smiling	Y.	Egret
Z.	Chasing	Z.	Bunny

NAMES FOR BOYS

First Name:		Last Name:	
A.	Powerful	A.	Prairie Dog
B.	Running	B.	Eagle
C.	Silent	C.	Manatee
D.	Brave	D.	Bobcat
E.	Proud	E.	Hedgehog
F.	Jumping	F.	Opossum
G.	Vanishing	G.	Panther
H.	Curious	H.	Snake
I.	Mighty	I.	Coyote
J.	Charging	J.	Ground Hog
K.	Handsome	K.	Rabbit
L.	Painted	L.	Iguana
M.	Poking	M.	Salamander
N.	Racing	N.	Alligator
O.	Helpful	O.	Bat
P.	Fierce	P.	Gopher
Q.	Strong	Q.	Shark
R.	Conquering	R.	Horse
S.	Lively	S.	Wolf
T.	Witty	T.	Aardvark
U.	Courageous	U.	Squirrel
V.	Honorable	V.	Beaver
W.	Rushing	W.	Raccoon
X.	Whispering	X.	Turtle
Y.	Eager	Y.	Armadillo
Z.	Thundering	Z.	Crocodile

Portal to Florida's Past
Magical Park

Junior Archaeologist Award

This award is for your outstanding achievement on the archaeology field trip.

Presented to:

_____   _____
Spirit Name   Your Name

Signed: Alligator With Large Pointy Teeth

Garry Walter

Use this to make a copy

37

ACTIVITY: BOOK QUESTIONS

Answer the following questions from the book.

1. What is a palmetto hut?

   _____

2. What is a palmetto hut made of?

   _____

3. What is a post mold?

   _____

4. What is a midden?

   _____

5. What is a burial mound?

   _____

6. What is an atlatl and what was it used for?

   _____

7. How was a dugout canoe made?

   _____

8. How did the native people make a fire?

   _____

9. How do archaeologists date objects?

   _____

10. What did the native people use for tools?

   _____

Appendix

GLOSSARY

1. **ancient:** from a long time ago

2. **archaeologist:** a scientist who studies artifacts from people long ago

3. **artifacts:** an object made or changed by human hands

4. **atlatl:** pole that holds a spear, used for hunting

5. **Calusa:** a group of people who lived in Florida 1600-400 years ago

6. **ceremony:** a special event or custom to celebrate together

7. **climate:** referring to the weather pattern of an area

8. **cordage:** rope, cord or twine made from natural fibers

9. **culture:** a way of life

10. **custom:** the way people do things in a group

11. **dig site:** an area used by archaeologists to learn about the past

12. **dugout canoe:** a boat dug out of a tree trunk

13. **environment:** everything that surrounds you

14. **extinct:** no longer living

15. **fossil:** minerals that replace a cell and crystallize (harden)

16. **grid:** an area of space that is separated by lines to form squares.

17. **mangrove:** trees that live in tropical climates along the shore and protect nature and shoreline

18. **midden:** a trash heap

19. **museum:** a place where a collection of objects are preserved

20. **natural resource:** something found in nature that people can use, like fresh water in Florida, which is what made it possible for prehistoric people to live here

21. **Paleoindians:** the first prehistoric people to live in North and South America, named by archaeologists

22. **paleontology:** the study of prehistoric life using fossils

23. **palmetto hut:** circular homes built by the prehistoric people

24. **potsherd:** pieces of broken pottery found on an archaeological site

25. **prehistoric:** a time before history was recorded by writing

26. **preserved:** kept or saved

27. **resources:** something that people use to live

28. **sea level:** the height of the ocean's surface

29. **timeline:** a diagram that shows events and when they took place

30. **tools:** archaeologists use tools to dig and measure

AL'S TIPS: Here is an easy way to remember the meaning of **ARCHAEOLOGY:**
The study of **ancient** human **activity** through **artifacts**.
Archaeology begins with an "A" and so does **ancient, activity** and **artifacts**.

AL'S TIPS: Here is an easy way to remember the meaning of **PALEONTOLOGY:**
The study of **prehistoric** life using fossils.
Paleontology begins with a "P" and so does **prehistoric**.

WORD SEARCH
Answer Page

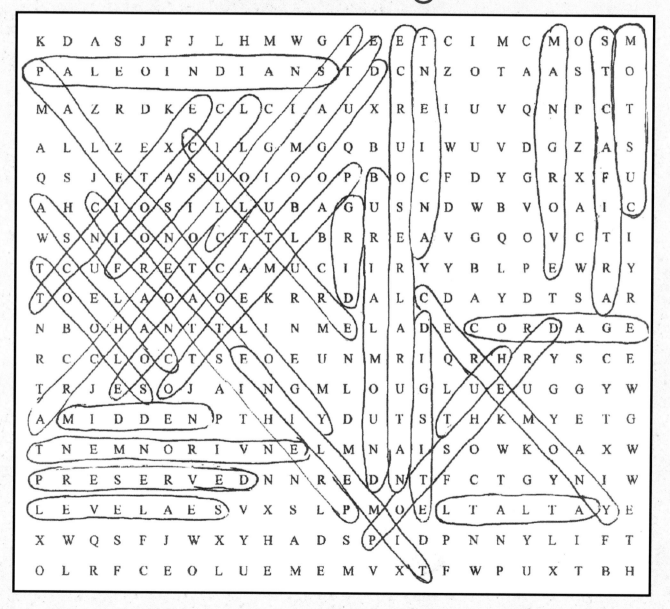

CROSSWORD PUZZLE
Answer Page

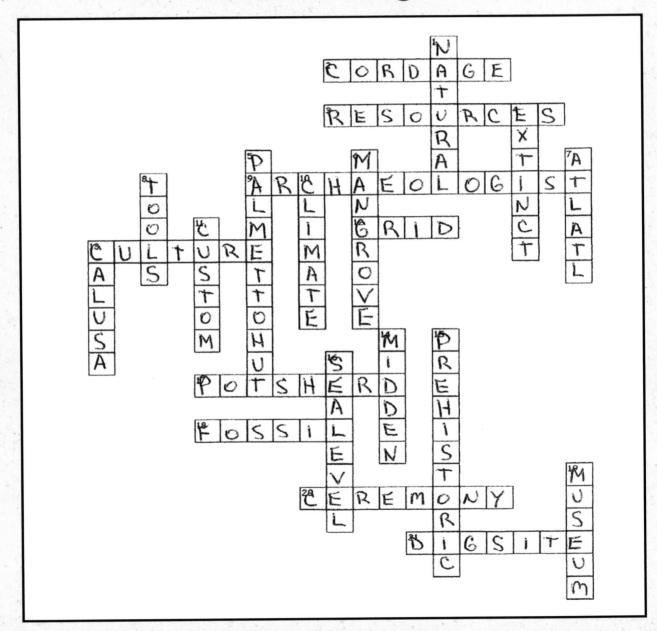

ARTIFACT SCAVENGER HUNT
Answer Page

 1. Whelk shell tool hammer.

 5. Turtle shell rattle.

 2. Clam shell scraper.

 6. Antler digging and scraping tool.

 3. Potsherd.

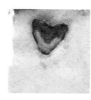 7. Shark tooth used for cutting and weapons.

 4. Jaw bone cutting tool.

 8. Fish vertebrae for jewelry.

TOOL SCAVENGER HUNT
Answer Page

1. A Total Station - telescope on a tripod used to map the site. It measures location and height of an artifact you are studying in a dig site.

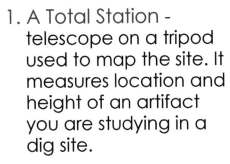

2. Sifting Screen - finding small artifacts buried in the soil of the dig site.

3. Small Shovel - removing soil around suspected artifact.

4. Brush - finer cleaning of artifact.

5. Ruler - measuring the size of a found artifact.

6. Paper - recording your dig site finds.

7. Pencil - writing.

8. Water Bottle - excavating a dig site is hard work. Staying hydrated is important.

9. Junior Archaeologist Certificate - a document of your accomplishment.

Parent and Teacher Guide

SUNSHINE STATE STANDARDS SOCIAL STUDIES GRADES 3-5

Grade Level Expectations
Social Studies Grades 3-5
Florida Department of Education
1
Standard A: Time, Continuity, and Change [History]
Standard 1: The student understands historical chronology and the historical perspective.
Benchmark SS.A.1.2.1: The student understands how individuals, ideas, decisions, and events can influence history.
Third
1. knows sources of information about ancient history (for example, books, magazines, documents at the school and community library, Internet sites about ancient history).
Fourth
1. knows different types of primary and secondary sources (for example, artifacts, diaries, letters, photographs, art, documents, newspapers, books, Internet sites about Florida history).
Fifth
Content addressed in third and fourth grade.
2
Benchmark SS.A.1.2.3: The student understands broad categories of time in years, decades, and centuries.
Grade Level Expectations
The student:
Third
1. reads and interprets a single timeline identifying the order of events (for example, in ancient times).
Fourth

Content addressed in Florida history (SS.A.6.2.1-7.)
Fifth
1. constructs and labels a timeline based on a historical reading (for example, about United States history).
Grade Level Expectations
The student:
Third
1. knows significant scientific and technological achievements of various societies (for example, bow and arrow, pottery, Egyptian pyramids).
Fourth
1. Content addressed in third grade.
Fifth
1. Content addressed in third grade.
Sunshine State Standards
Grade Level Expectations
Social Studies
Grades 3-5
18
Benchmark SS.A.6.2.6: The student understands the cultural, social, and political features of Native American tribes in Florida's history.
Grade Level Expectations
The student:
Third
Content addressed in fourth grade.
Fourth
1. understands selected aspects of the cultural, social, and political features of Native American tribes in the history of Florida.
Fifth
Content addressed in fourth grade.

About the Author

Photo by Ellen Di Piazza

Amy Elder earned her Bachelor of Science in Business Administration from Boston University, a Master of Education from Lesley College and a Master of Arts in Library and Information Science from the University of South Florida. She has lived in Osprey, Florida, since 1995. She started writing professionally when she moved to Florida.

Elder has written and published two history books called, *Images of America: Sarasota* and *Images of America: Sarasota 1940-2005*. She has won two book awards from the National League of American Pen Women state competition, first place for her history book, *Images of America: Sarasota 1940-2005* and first place for her educational children's book, *Under the Sea from A to Z*.

For the past several years, Elder has worked as a judge for the National League of American Pen Women College Scholarship Program. She has worked directly with the six public high schools in Sarasota, Florida, to help promote writing with local youth. Besides reading, judging and communicating with teachers and seniors, she has raised money for the program through a silent auction and worked as a mentor.

Elder has taught for many years, worked as a high school media specialist and was a reference librarian at New College for five years before teaching at Historic Spanish Point. She describes walking on the shell paths at Spanish Point as stepping back 100 years in history. She loves this special place and wants to help preserve and take care of it for the next generations. When she is not teaching or writing, she enjoys sailing on the Gulf of Mexico with her husband, son and dog.

About the Illustrator

Garry Walter was born in the foothills of the Allegheny Mountains in Pennsylvania, where he earned his Associates Degree in Specialized Technology. He has been an air conditioning contractor for 30 years. He has lived in Florida since 1979, where he designs, sells and teaches historical crafting to living history museums. Locally Garry, with his wife Cindy, are affiliated with Historic Spanish Point, working with school groups. He has always had an interest in old structures and wildlife which he interprets through paintings in watercolor and drawings in pencil.

Garry has studied painting with many recognized oil impressionists. He has furthered his education with nationally renowned watercolor and pencil sketch artists. His work is on display at local art galleries as well as several wildlife refuges and the Audubon House in Key West. Recently some of his wildlife artwork were selected as set props for the movie Dolphin Tale. They are on display at the Clearwater Marine Aquarium, where the movie was filmed.

Currently one of his watercolor paintings is featured on the summer cover of The Peppertree Press, a quarterly magazine for book publication. You can see more of Garry's artwork, or contact him at www.OldeTymeArtsAndCrafts.com

CPSIA information can be obtained at www.ICGtesting.com
Printed in the USA
LVIW01n0826120516
487909LV00005B/7